Face Food Recipes
© 2009 by Christopher D Salyers

Concept, design and words: Christopher D Salyers
Japanese translations and assistance: Eri Hamaji

Typeset in Ultramagnetic

Library of Congress Control #2009933497

Printed and bound in China through Asia Pacific Offset

10 9 8 7 6 5 4 3 2 1   First edition

Mark Batty Publisher
36 West 37th Street, Suite 409
New York, NY 10018

www.markbattypublisher.com

ISBN-13: 978-0-9819600-2-9

Distributed outside North America by:

Thames & Hudson Ltd
181A High Holborn
London WC1V 7QX
United Kingdom
Tel: 00 44 20 7845 5000
Fax: 00 44 20 7845 5055
www.thameshudson.co.uk

フェイスフードレシピ

FACE FOOD RECIPES

A HOW-TO GUIDE BY CHRISTOPHER D SALYERS

クリストファー・D・サルヤーズによる実用書

協力：濱地絵里 WITH ERI HAMAJI

MARK BATTY PUBLISHER
NEW YORK CITY
マークバティー出版社
米国・ニューヨーク市

TABLE OF
CONTENTS
もくじ

INTRODUCTION
はじめに

From an early age, I cultivated a special relationship with cleverly molded, prepackaged food. It all began with my first chocolate Easter bunny at the impressionable age of one. In time, I discovered French-fried potato dinosaurs, crackers posing as animals, alphabet pasta and cereal shaped like fruit—each satisfying my desire for fun alternatives to conventional foods. It doesn't have to be all bad for you, of course. It was only a matter of time before someone moved this whimsical notion in a healthier direction. Credit goes to Japanese mothers. Welcome to the world of *charaben*. Welcome to *Face Food Recipes*.

Charaben (or *kyaraben*) is a portmanteau—a merging or fusion—of "character" and "bento," a fresh Japanese trend that really is just that: adorable likenesses molded from rice, cut out of seaweed or formed with ham. The origin of *charaben* isn't clearly defined, but only because, at the youthful age of ten, its popularity is so new. Of the mothers and fathers I've spoken with, including those who crafted the *charaben* you'll see in this book, none began making them before the ball dropped on the year 2000.* All attribute *charaben's* widespread appeal to the internet and online social networking forums, and most enthusiasts (like myself) fell in love with a single image and then felt their infatuation steamroll from there. Like any hobby, *charaben* seeks perfection in comparison, so mothers and fathers started photographing their creations before handing them off to their children—a flash of digital documentation to mill over, study and define. Pictures are uploaded, websites and blogs take shape and before even a year passes a network of parents across Japan have connected, all obsessed with the idea of turning their children's lunches into something more: the character bento.

Quite a few things changed in the two years that passed since my last visit to Tokyo. There's now a *charaben* Wikipedia page, for one. An eighteen-meter tall, "life-size" statue of Gundam (an anime *mecha*, or giant robot) now towers over the artificial island of Odaiba, at the ready for any *kaiju* battle that might threaten the city. I was called *gaijin* only once during my entire stay—a remarkable testament to the times in and of itself.

As the Japanese economy has slowed a bit, appreciation has risen for the well-constructed bento. Even Japanese salarymen felt the pinch—no longer is it bad form for a man to pack his lunch. The art of the bento, a tradition that dates as far back as the Kamakura period (1185-1333) when pre-cooked rice was first developed, has clean and defined beginnings. It was street food or a meal to be eaten during a *humami*. It wasn't until the 1980s that the bento boom really kicked in, but many salarymen saw these polystyrene boxes as subpar status symbols, opting instead for the daily suit-set of cigarettes, restaurant fare and a steady stream of beer.

Not to say that there's anything wrong with that, but a well-packaged lunch is a healthier one: fewer preservatives, the pleasure of a home-prepped meal, a growing bank account as opposed to an expanding waistline. Apprehensive over the swarming invasion of fast food chains like KFC, Wendy's and McDonald's, the new Japanese intelligentsia is bringing the bento back to its roots: a clean, healthy, affordable alternative to the grab-n-go lunch. Bento boxes are no longer stacked up in stores, emblazoned with childish logos and in bright colors—well, those are still there, of course, but sleek, black bento boxes are also more widely available, with brands targeting men who'd like to maintain that Axe Body Spray aesthetic.

*I suspect that the trend really started around the mid 1990s, during anime's international boom.

Takkun, son of TakuPapa, thrills over our table of *charaben*.

Peering through the framework of society's conditions, the only question I can ask myself is: What man wouldn't take a bento made by one of the many contributors of this book? So much has changed since last we met.

Nico* has moved out of her flat into the second level of a modern townhouse. No longer is she that delicate house mom in her too-small-yet-too-cute apartment, the budding spokeswoman for all things humble and approachable. No, this Nico wears a tanktop and walks with a swagger, an oversized black beanie covering bleached-blonde locks. She had little time for me but was eager to share her *charaben*, which I snatched up immediately and claimed as my own. Her son had that locked gaze of curiosity so prevalent in young boys, no matter where they are in this world. He was loud. He referred to me as a "big boy" and said I was *sugoi*, behaving as if Himura Kenshin had walked into the room.

*See pages 60–63

Sayuri Kubo's verve left me dizzy with her highbrow take on Alphonse Mucha's "Laurel," a delicate yet striking image that I chose to make the mascot of this entire project. You'll know her bentos when you see them. I'm in absolute awe of her.

Muku* took the first *Face Food* and ran with it. Petite, perky and an accomplished cook, Muku is now a minor celeb in the Japanese *charaben* world. Her bentos have made the rounds and she is now the proud author of her own set of cookbooks. The other mothers asked for her autograph during our meetings. The air around us was different.

Did I mention that there are now multiple English-language *charaben* books? Does *Face Food* get honorable mention for being the first kid on the block?

The *charaben* craze began as an adorable method to convince children to eat healthier—because if it looks cool they're

*See pages 16–17

likely to put it in their mouths, or so the logic goes. Now many are seeing this trend make a strange shift, with food artificiality lapping health and design trumping all else. Children regard these meals as toys. In turn, many schools have placed a ban on *charaben* inside the cafeteria. A few mothers I met with even claimed that the trend was on a downward trajectory. How Japan-centric.

As with any chic, new thing, *charaben* hasn't seen its glory days, nor has it seen its finest genius. The Yokohama *Charaben* Contest continues on, as does the Sanrio *Charaben* Contest, which as of 2010 is in its fourth year. New talents emerge and more content makes it onto the airwaves: there's the uber-prolific Gurea; Sauth, another father in the company of many mothers; and Obacchi, who is young and

hip and only makes *jacketben* from the albums of bands she likes, refusing to slice seaweed into anything else. (Go ahead and ask her—I tried.) So, just as the established refine their art, the newbies bring fresh ideas and leftfield concepts to the *charaben* world.

When crafting your bento, keep the food in mind as you build your shapes—nutrition, taste and design should all rank equally. Use the images and the illustrated guides as cheat sheets for your own creations. Now turn the page and pick out your tools. Take what you see in this book and, as with all experiments, just roll with it.

Cars by Mariko Nihei;
Anpanman by Risa Takizawa

CHARABEN
TOOLS
キャラ弁作りの道具たち

The tools of the *charaben* trade.

USE WHAT YOU FIND IN YOUR KITCHEN

When the phenomenon first took off, *charaben* were made with typical kitchen tools combined with some arts and crafts know-how. Sometimes it's the simplest thing, like an X-Acto knife or razor blade, that'll do everything you need done within the confines of your bento box. But everyone has their own methods and their own toolbox full of surprises. Gurea*, for instance, opts for a needle over a razor blade when she's slicing delicate shapes for details cast in cheese. Risa Takizawa (her Anpanman is pictured on page 9) lists her essential tools as: "eyebrow scissors (to cut seaweed), tweezers (to position small parts), straws of various sizes (to make small circles out of cheese, fish cake and ham) and a plastic capsule (to make round shapes)." There isn't exactly a "*charaben* starter kit" (though a few overpriced packages come close), so take one step back and think of inventive ways to sculpt and mold food. (I frequently visit both my desk drawer and toolbox for ideas.)

RAZOR BLADE (or X-Acto knife): This is used mainly for carving out details from nori—facial features, shadows, outlines, hair—and some take this one step further by slicing complex shapes to make their own unique pieces of seaweed art—popular in the Japanese bento world. Personally, I like a basic razor blade, but many opt for an X-Acto with a handle and curved blade.

HOLE PUNCH: This might seem unappealing to some (who wants to bring the office into the kitchen?) but, really, a hole punch can come in handy. Eyes (open or closed), eyebrows or any small, curved shape can be punched out of your nori with ease.

SCISSORS: I use three different sizes, the smallest taken from a sewing kit, the next size up made especially for delicate food.

SMALL KNIFE: Sometimes the most basic tool is the most essential. I'm comfortable with my fruit knife and use it often, even with *charaben*.

*See pages 13, 35, 38–39, 54–57, 64–65

MEASURING TAPE: This is to be used only in extreme circumstances, namely when my patience for perfection has worn itself thin or when the *charaben* feels too complex for my tired eyes.

CHOPSTICKS: Used to move, place and adjust food in the bento. I buy these in bulk.

COOKIE CUTTERS: Generic cookie cutters can be bought in just about any kitchenware store and work wonders turning cheese, egg or sliced meat into stars, hearts and cute round faces. Only a few are pictured in the photograph but I own a large tin's worth of shapes.

OTHER NECESSARY ITEMS INCLUDE:

STRAWS: When the hole punch feels like too much, these make simple eyes out of softer solid foods like cheese or steamed vegetables.

PLASTIC BOTTLES: An inexpensive and readily available alternative to the cookie cutter. Take a regular plastic bottle (size depends on the desired effect, but anything will do) and cut a circular band out of its midsection. Because it's thin plastic, this form doesn't have to stay a circle—it can be bent, cut or twisted into any shape you choose. Alternatively, lids, caps and jars make excellent form cutters because they vary. The general rule of thumb is to never waste and always keep your imagination on the *charaben*.

TOOTHPICKS: The oft-underappreciated item stuck next to your spices. Toothpicks make great mini chopsticks, can be used for stippling and applying the smallest dab of mayo for "glue."

SARAN WRAP: This is perfect for when you're cutting and assembling your character on a seperate surface (like a cutting board) and must transfer it to your bento box. Saran wrap is also useful to have wrapped beneath the lid of your bento to keep its contents from shifting too much in transit.

TRACING PAPER: When your sketch is too complicated to eyeball, simply trace it.

WHAT YOU FIND IN STORES

The Japanese love their appliances—heck, most of the world loves a great kitchen gadget or twelve (Ronco, anyone?), and products marketed for *charaben*-making are no exception. From websites devoted specifically to *charaben* tools to their own aisle at Tokyu Hands, the mass-produced items used to craft *charaben* can be useless, uber-cute, an absolute time-saver or nothing more than overpriced alternatives to ordinary kitchen items you already own—their true *charaben* purposes yet undiscovered. Though your first inclination may be to attack these with full-on *kawaii* enthusiasm, I'd advise you to use creative restraint when shelling out cash for *charaben* tools.

Nori punchers might be one item worth your yen. They're a favorite of mine, since the eyes and mouths of characters tend to take up that little bit of time best spent on something else. A number of specific *charaben* nori-punch sets are out on the market, but the average arts-and-crafts decorative hole punch works just as well. Truly dedicated *charaben* artisans, like Muku, stress: "I don't use hole punchers or cookie cutters. I try to make *charaben*s with only simple tools and techniques." However, it's more common to use tools to cheat in your kitchen—go ahead, I won't tell. Sauce "pens" are handy, too, for when you want to spread something (like mayo, for glue) over delicate paths, or when you'd like to write a message to that special someone. Condiment containers also come in many shapes and likenesses, but experience says these are more form than function. You can also find molders for rice in many different and useful shapes, including brand-name molds of many internationally known characters like Hello Kitty, Doraemon and everything Disney. Again, *charaben*-specific scissors, tweezers and the like are really overpriced versions of common household items.

HOW TO USE THIS BOOK TO MAKE A *CHARABEN*

This book can't give you the skills needed to intricately slice seaweed with a razor blade, mold rice with your hands or even fry the perfect egg sheet. What this book does show you, however, is a complete breakdown of each *charaben*'s ingredients using a simple paint-by-numbers illustration. I then (where it's warranted) give a brief line or two outlining the process. It can seem easy on paper but, really, it's all art.

Note the face below for instance: Ground sesame seeds make up his "hair" while the eyes, lips and whiskers are sliced out of

nori. The rest of him—the rice—is molded by hand. Think you can do it?

Each recipe in this book breaks down the *charaben* into its most basic ingredients. The rest of the bento is accented with what I refer to as "garnish," the attractively placed and edible extras you select to fill your bento. It's up to you what to put there.

There is basic bento knowledge that may be unfamiliar to some. What is nori, for instance? Ok, that's an obvious one, but it's answered in the glossary in case you don't know. You can also turn to the glossary for techniques on rice preparation, instructions on how to make an authentic Japanese "hamburg" or how to dye rice and eggs. It's all there to get you started on your first *charaben* experience.

If you need some assistance, log on to www.markbattypublisher.com to download sketch templates from the book, as well as never-before-seen *charaben* designs. (Hint: print these straight to tracing paper!)

This nerdy *onigiri* (by Gurea) is a cute reminder of how we see faces in everything, even our food.

Red Pink

white

Pink & Yellow

Red

whi.

Alphonse Mucha 月桂樹.

Laurel

Sayura Kubo's original sketch for Alphonse Mucha's "Laurel."
See the final product on page 22.

FACE FOOD
RECIPES

フェイスフードレシピ

Sharaku 東洲斎写楽

by Muku

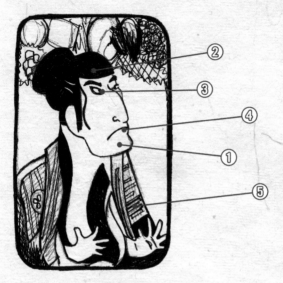

TOSHUSAI SHARAKU WOODBLOCK PRINT

1. fish cake
2. fish cake, nori
3. seaweed, fish cake, imitation crab
4. nori
5. salami, imitation crab, spinach, nori

Sharaku* is one of the great Japanese masters of woodblock printing, active only briefly (1794–1795) during the Edo period. Muku pays homage with this *charaben*, maintaining the artist's distinctly personal kabuki aesthetic.

To begin, sketch the illustration on tracing paper, which you'll use as a guide for cutting. Think in layers: for the eyes it's the imitation crab, then the fish cake, then the nori. The detail is intricate on this one, so it may take a few attempts.

*Though mainly a theory, some maintain that a real Sharaku never existed. Instead, the name was taken from *sharakusai*, "nonsense," and was used as a joke among artists who worked collectively, factory-like, under the suggestive moniker.

One Piece ワンピース

by Mihochin

MONKEY D. LUFFY AND CHOPPER OF ONE PIECE

1. ham
2. seaweed
3. egg yolk
4. egg dyed with brown sugar
5. fish cake, seaweed
6. imitation crab
7. ham, fish cake
8. fish cake dyed with blue food coloring

Mihochin's *charaben* was inspired by the anime and bestselling *Weekly Shonen Jump* manga *One Piece*. Featured is the main character, Monkey D. Luffy, an energetic, wannabe pirate sailing the seas in search of a lost, legendary treasure.

First, lay a bed of lettuce and flatten white rice evenly across the leaves. Use a blade to carve your shapes on a cutting board. It's recommended that you use a sketch on tracing paper for the hair, or to size up the heads in order to achieve proper dimensions.

Mice Rice ねずみちゃんのタコライス

by Akinoichigo

② ① ③

TWO FRENCHY EGG MOUSERS

1. hard boiled egg
2. ham
3. nori

Akinoichigo's pair rests delicately on a salad of lettuce, onion, tomato, carrot and chicken *soboro*. The French-labeled bento box is a nod to the bilateral relations between these two countries, a love affair that dates back to the seventeenth century, when the samurai diplomat Hasekura Rokuemon Tsunenaga became a sensation in Saint-Tropez.

Cut slits into your boiled egg, trim your ham and then attach using mayonnaise.

Alphonse Mucha

アルフォンス・ミュシャ

by Sayuri Kubo

ALPHONSE MUCHA'S "LAUREL"

1. ham
2. fried fish cake
3. imitation crab
4. fish cake, imitation crab
5. nori

Alphonse Mucha was a Czech artist and popular inspiration for the art nouveau style, actively producing posters, paintings and illustrations as well as jewelry and set designs in Paris at the end of the nineteenth century.

Sayuri's take on the original lithograph is a very Japanese one: lost are her sunken eyes and suggestive smirk.

Much like Mucha, Kubo maintained an earthy, natural palette by adding okra, egg, broccoli, bean noodles, cod roe, shrimp and chicken to the bento.

Very Hungry Caterpillar

はらぺこあおむし

by Mihochin

THE SCARED (BUT HUNGRY) CATERPILLAR

1. green beans
2. sausage
3. egg, lettuce
4. seaweed
5. seaweed

The tubular, segmented body of the caterpillar is a favorite among predators for its high protein content. This little guy, however, is a little more appealing to us humans.

Mihochin also includes an agreeable assortment of colors in her add-ons of meatball, broccoli, cherry tomato, fried egg with shrimp, beef-wrapped green beans and lettuce.

Honeybees ミツバチ

by Maki Ogawa

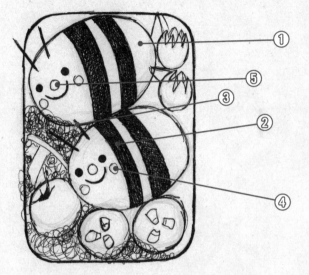

TWO HONEYBEES IN A BENTO

1. rice dyed with curry
2. nori
3. pretzel sticks
4. thinly sliced tomato
5. ham

The world's largest hornet is the Japanese sparrow bee, 50 mm in length with a wingspan of 76 mm. That's about the size of an adult thumb! Maki Ogawa's bees are even bigger but much easier to digest.

"*Charaben* are about food rather than amusement," Maki says. "I stay aware of the fact that it should be a healthy lunch, one that doesn't sacrifice nutrition or rely heavily on artificial foods just to make it look good."

Dragon Ball ドラゴンボール

by Mihochin

GOHAN AND GOKU FROM DRAGON BALL Z

1. ham
2. nori
3. fish cake and nori
4. egg dyed with ketchup
5. boiled spinach
6. egg yolk
7. fish cake

Dragon Ball is one of the most popular manga/anime series of all time, both in Japan and abroad. The story centers around Goku, a monkey-tailed boy on a quest to recover the seven scattered dragon balls (and defend Earth using his insane martial arts).

Gohan is Goku's son, and Mihochin has captured the likenesses of both in strik-ingly accurate detail, spread across a row of sandwiches.

If you're going to get anything right with this *charaben*, make sure it's the hair. Mihochin made sandwiches of three varieties: egg and mayo, cheddar and cucumber, American cheese and smoked ham. She garnishes with green beans, lettuce, sausage and cherry tomatoes.

Legend of Zelda ゼルダの伝説

by TakuPapa

LINK FROM THE LEGEND OF ZELDA

1. egg dyed with spinach powder
2. cheese
3. ham
4. egg yolk
5. nori, fish cake
6. nori, egg yolk
7. nori, fish cake
8. ham, seaweed, red pepper, fish cake

The first *Zelda* video game was released in 1986 on the Nintendo Famicom Game System. A role-playing game set in a fantastical realm called Hyrule, *Zelda* was inspired by creator Shigeru Miyamoto's own childhood explorations in Kyoto.

"I know five *charaben* fathers," TakuPapa says. "There must be more out there. The number is growing."

30

Panda Party パンダパーティー

by Akinoichigo

PANDA PARTY IN A BENTO

1. rice
2. nori

These expressive little guys make for a great starter *charaben*. The bears are made from rice balls and sliced nori. Garnish as you please—Akinoichigo opted for baby corn, *tamago*, sausage, sliced carrot and... a little panda candy!

Akinoichigo sees the *charaben* trend shifting to what some call *decoben*, bentos made by Japanese housewives that are "less fancy than *charaben* and just a little bit decorative and cute."

Dokaben ドカベン

by TakuPapa

TARO YAMADA FROM DOKABEN

1. rice paper
2. fish cake
3. ham
4. rice paper dyed with spinach powder
5. nori

Since its introduction in 1872, baseball has remained one of the most popular sports in Japan. Anime/manga series like *Dokaben*, *Touch* and *Rookies* are quite popular, second only to the hugely successful basketball series *Slam Dunk*.

A *dokaben* is a large-sized bento—a favorite of the series' protagonist, Taro Yamada.

GeGeGe no Kitaro ゲゲゲの鬼太郎

by Gurea

KITARO OF THE GRAVEYARD BENTO

1. thinly fried egg dyed with brown sugar
2. rice, salmon flakes
3. fish cake, nori
4. nori
5. boiled quail egg, imitation crab, nori
6. carrot, pork
7. fish cake, imitation crab
8. fish sausage

Adapted from an early twentieth-century Japanese folk tale performed as *kamishibai* (meaning "paper drama"), *GeGeGe*'s very *kawaii*, goth-like *yokai* ("spirit monster") has been popularized through manga, anime and even live-action film.

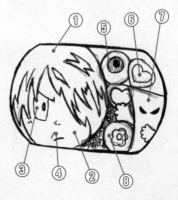

Mayo Family 親子で夏休みマヨネーズ

by TakuPapa

KEWPIE MAYONNAISE

1. egg, ham, rice
2. cheese
3. sliced red pepper
4. nori

Kewpie Mayonnaise is a popular name brand of mayo in Japan, famous for the Kewpie doll icon on its packaging. TakuPapa dropped the babydoll and instead created characters of the bottles themselves in this utterly original *charaben*.

Rilakkuma リラックマ

by Akiko Wakabayashi

RILAKKUMA AND KORILAKKUMA

1. fried bean curd
2. egg
3. fish cake
4. potato
5. ham
6. nori

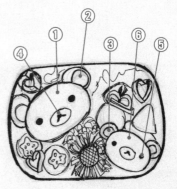

Rilakkuma is a bear who, true to his name (a combination of the Japanese pronunciation of "relax" and the Japanese word for bear), likes to watch clothes dry. His favorite foods are pancakes, dumplings and doughnuts, so chances are he wouldn't eat this *charaben*. Filling out the bento is some pasta, okra, sausage, cherry tomato, sweet yam and lettuce.

Usarusan うさるさん

by Gurea

A BUNNY BENTO

1. fried bean curd
2. rice
3. sliced tomato
4. nori
5. fish sausage, black sesame

An ordinary male rabbit that can transform into Usarusan by wearing a monkey costume and eating bananas. *Kawaii!* His name is a combination of *usagi* (rabbit) and *saru* (monkey).

Gurea used a sprinkling of *denbu* (pink fish powder) to add blush to the cheeks.

Astro Boy 鉄腕アトム

by Gurea

MIGHTY ATOM

1. ham
2. nori
3. nori
4. egg yolk, imitation crab
5. fish cake, nori

Astro Boy is manga/anime series about a little robotic boy, Astro, who was built by Doctor Tenma after his real son died in a car accident.

Nothing beats the original black-and-white cartoon, not even its new Hollywood CGI counterpart.

Pokemon 1 ポケモン

by Goma

GIZAMIMI PICHU AND PICHU

1. egg (with little yolk)
2. egg (with extra yolk)
3. ham
4. red sausage
5. nori
6. nori
7. ham
8. fishcake, nori

Pokemon is a romanized contraction of the Japanese brand *Pocket Monsters*, and in 1997 hundreds of children were hospitalized with epileptic seizures, caused by the red and blue strobing lights in the episode "Electric Soldier Porygon." The most this bento will give you is, perhaps, indigestion.

Care Bears ケアーベア

by Kaerenmama

A BENTO KINGDOM OF CARING

1. **rice dyed with food coloring**
2. **nori**
3. **carrot**
4. **hotdog**

My favorite was Grumpy Bear, who had the image of a rain cloud on his belly. Watching them as a child I often wondered: Were they born this way or did they tattoo each other based on mood?

These two bears are formed with rice and... tons of love.

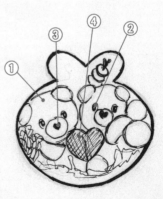

Pirates! 海賊

by Maki Ogawa

PIRATE BALLS AND BOOTY

1. rice
2. nori
3. nori
4. ham

I don't think this little guy is going to hijack a boat anytime soon...

If you're going to experiment with recipes, this is another excellent *charaben* to start with since the ingredients are few and the design is based on the simple rice ball.

"I practice cooking daily and study good design," says Maki. "I get hints from paintings, photographs, illustrated books and general cookbooks."

The Velvet Underground

ベルベット・アンダーグラウンド

by Obacchi

THE VELVET UNDERGROUND & NICO

1. rice
2. egg
3. nori

One of Andy Warhol's most iconic images is this peel-able album cover for the band's debut, seen here in all its *charaben* glory. Obacchi is an expert in seaweed art, working exclusively on what she calls *jacketben* or *charaben* of record album covers.

Using the original art as a guide, cut the banana out of fried egg. Place the banana on top of white rice. Use an X-Acto knife to slice your nori, but be patient as type can be difficult to master.

Little Tikes リトルタイクス

by Akinoichigo

TIKES WITH AMERICAN PRIDE

1. imitation crab
2. egg dyed with brown sugar
3. egg dyed with spinach powder
4. egg
5. seaweed
6. egg white
7. cheese
8. ham

American toys for toddlers (or nostalgic adults) make their *charaben* debut. Akinoichigo spread these little rugrats over sandwiches, cutting delicate nori facial features for each.

Ponyo 崖の上のポニョ

by Sauth

PONYO FLOATING DOWNSTREAM

1. egg dyed with ketchup
2. ham
3. egg whites
4. imitation crab
5. nori

Ponyo is the latest animated craze from Studio Ghibli, written and directed by Hayao Miyazaki (of *Princess Mononoke* fame), about a goldfish named Ponyo who befriends a five-year-old human boy and wishes to become a human girl.

After cutting and layering his ingredients into a Ponyo, Sauth accented this bento with a sausage-and-broccoli flower and some funny-shaped pasta.

A Teddy Holiday

くまさんのクリスマス

by Maki Ogawa

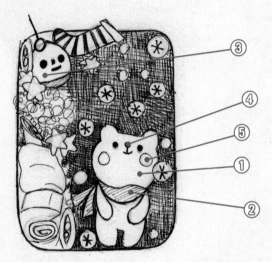

A TEDDY BEAR CHRISTMAS

1. egg
2. imitation crab
3. quail egg
4. nori
5. imitation crab

I have two teddy bears from two major Christmases in my life: "Buttons" was handmade by my grandmother and given to me on my first Christmas; "Teddy" is bigger, browner and more mature, as he was given to me for Christmas number five. Though you can't sew a button on this little bear if he loses an eye, it's okay: you're better off eating it all anyway.

Maki first lined her bento with white rice, then used nori over top for the nighttime effect. The circular bits of white for the snowflakes were cut from potatoes using a knife.

Bleach ブリーチ

by Mihochin

①
③
②
⑤
④

ICHIGO KUROSAKI FROM BLEACH

1. egg dyed with ketchup
2. ham
3. nori, egg white
4. egg white, cheese
5. nori

The TV series *Bleach* is a dark fantasy anime centered around the adventures of orange-haired Ichigo Kurosaki, a fifteen-year-old student who obtains the powers of *shinigami* (the "spirit of death" or Grim Reaper).

Mihochin is an expert when it comes to capturing the expressive details of anime. Ichigo is placed over bread, lettuce and some rolled-up ham. This is about as creative as a sandwich can get!

Drifters ドリフターズ

by Gurea

BAKA TONOSAMA AND KATOCHAN

1. rice dyed with ketchup
2. fish cake, nori
3. fish cake, nori, imitation crab
4. rice
5. nori

The Drifters is a comedy and musical duo best known for their long-running variety show *Hachijidayo, Zen'inshugo!* (*It's 8 p.m., Everyone Together!*) which aired from 1969–1985.

Gurea filled out this bento using tempura, strawberry, fish sausage, hot dog and fried egg.

Detective Conan
名探偵コナン

by Gurea

CASE CLOSED ON THIS BENTO

1. cheese, nori
2. ham
3. hot dog
4. fish cake dyed with purple cabbage
5. fish cake
6. ham
7. fish cake dyed with purple cabbage
8. nori

A seventeen-year-old detective in the body
of a seven-year-old. Such is the plot of
Detective Conan, an anime series starring
Jimmy Kudo as Conan Edogawa, a pseud-
onym blended from two detective authors:
Arthur Conan Doyle and Edogawa Rampo.

Japan Railways JR東日本

by Gurea

THE HAKONE STOP ON THE JR LINE

1. imitation crab, nori
2. nori
3. cheese, nori
4. fish cake dyed with purple cabbage and blue food coloring
5. broccoli
6. thin crepe dyed with green tea powder

The JR is one of seven railway companies in Japan and the largest in the world. Now all we need is a Suica penguin bento to match!

Note the use of broccoli for trees and the many colored pebbles. Such skill is nearly as efficient as the JR!

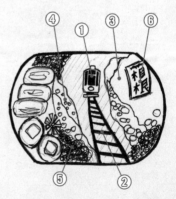

Kamen Rider 仮面ライダー

by Gurea

KAMEN RIDER STRONGER

1. red pepper
2. fish cake dyed with blue food coloring, cucumber
3. cheese, nori
4. egg, egg dyed with ketchup
5. thinly fried egg
6. sliced edamame
7. nori
8. fish cake

Kamen Rider began as a *tokusatsu* (live action "special effects") series in 1973. This spandex-wearing, grasshopper-like superhero battles the mutant cyborgs of "Shocker," an evil terrorist organization hellbent on world domination.

Hitman Reborn! ヒットマンリボーン！

by Blue

"TUNA" FROM HOME TUTOR HITMAN REBORN!

1. ham
2. thinly fried egg dyed with soy sauce, seasoned kelp
3. nose and mouth: fish cake, seaweed, thinly fried egg dyed with ketchup, fried egg white
4. thinly fried egg, thinly fried egg dyed with ketchup
5. fish cake, purple cabbage, seasoned kelp

"Tuna" is the nickname of protagonist Tsunayoshi Sawada from the bestselling *Weekly Shonen Jump* manga.

Guri & Gura ぐりとぐら

by Gurea

THE FIELD MICE

1. thinly fried egg dyed with brown rice
2. fish cake dyed with purple cabbage
3. thinly fried egg dyed with ketchup
4. thinly fried egg
5. nori

These human-like mice twins are from a series of classic illustrated children's books by Yuriko Omura.

Rodents that go on picnic adventures and teach children about cooking—so of course you would eat them, right?

Naruto 1 -ナルト-

by Nico

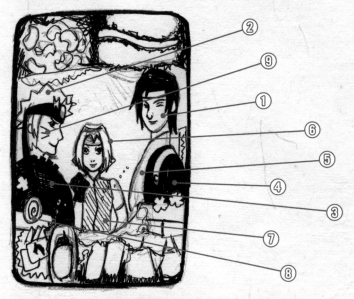

NARUTO UZUMAKI, SAKURA HARUNO & SAI

1. ham
2. egg yolk
3. seaweed
4. seaweed
5. rice paper
6. ham
7. egg dyed with food coloring
8. imitation crab, carrot
9. nori

Naruto is a popular manga/anime series about a simple adolescent ninja on a quest for fame and martial arts notoriety in his village.

Nico, once again summoning her inner chakra for *charaben* design, brings together the series' three main characters, highly detailed and expressive across a plain backdrop of white rice.

Nico achieved her bright red by dying egg with food coloring. The other components include pasta, lettuce, fried shrimp, lemon, rice and fried fish cake.

Naruto 2 -ナルト-

by Nico

SASUKE UCHIHA FROM NARUTO

1. seaweed
2. ham
3. egg white
4. nori
5. sausage, egg

Sasuke Uchiha is the foil to the series' titular character, Naruto. As Sasuke grew to be more empathetic towards his rival, fans jokingly labeled him as the anime's "emo kid."

Nico has a fantastic sense of color, lines and placement. She wrapped this bento in a delicious mix of green beans, egg, minced chicken, burdock, carrot, pork, edamame, lettuce, fish cake and rice.

Spiderman スパイダーマン

by Gurea

WEB–SLINGING SPIDEY

1. egg yolk dyed with ketchup
2. fish cake dyed with purple cabbage
3. fish cake
4. nori

Spiderman's big entry into pop–culture Japan was a weird and very un-Spiderman *tokusatsu* series that aired in the late seventies, alongside *Ultraman* and *Kamen Rider* (see page 57).

This *charaben* is an excellent example of how three-dimensional images can be achieved through a layering of ingredients.

Pokemon 2 ポケモン - トロピウス

by Goma

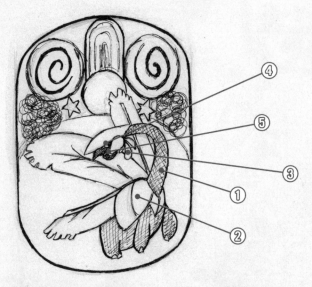

TROPIUS FROM POKEMON

1. thin crepe made by mixing flour, cocoa powder, sugar and water
2. thin crepe made by mixing flour, green tea powder, sugar and water
3. cheese
4. fish cake, nori
5. imitation crab

Tropius is identified as "a dual-type Grass/Flying Pokemon." I really have no idea what that means, but I do know that he enjoys fruit, which is totally absent from this bento.

Regarding process, Goma adds: "It's difficult to make the *charaben* so that they stay intact. I use mayo to attach parts or pin things with uncooked spaghetti."

Humpty Dumpty

ハンプティ・ダンプティ

by Sayuri Kubo

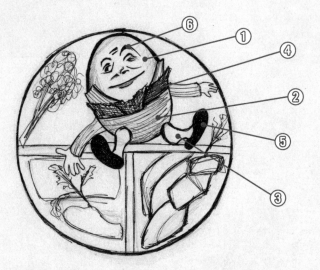

HUMPTY DUMPTY MADE A GREAT BENTO

1. hard boiled egg
2. imitation crab
3. fish cake
4. lettuce
5. nori
6. nori

A nursery rhyme character perhaps best remembered from Lewis Carroll's *Through the Looking-Glass*, where he shared with Alice his strange disdain for verbs.

This egg man is perched playfully atop a traditional bamboo bento box.

Kubo has been making *charaben* since 2005, when she came across the *gagben* (humor bentos) of Kasumin, a blogger who garnered large amounts of media attention in Japan.

Hello Kitty ハローキティ

by Mihochin

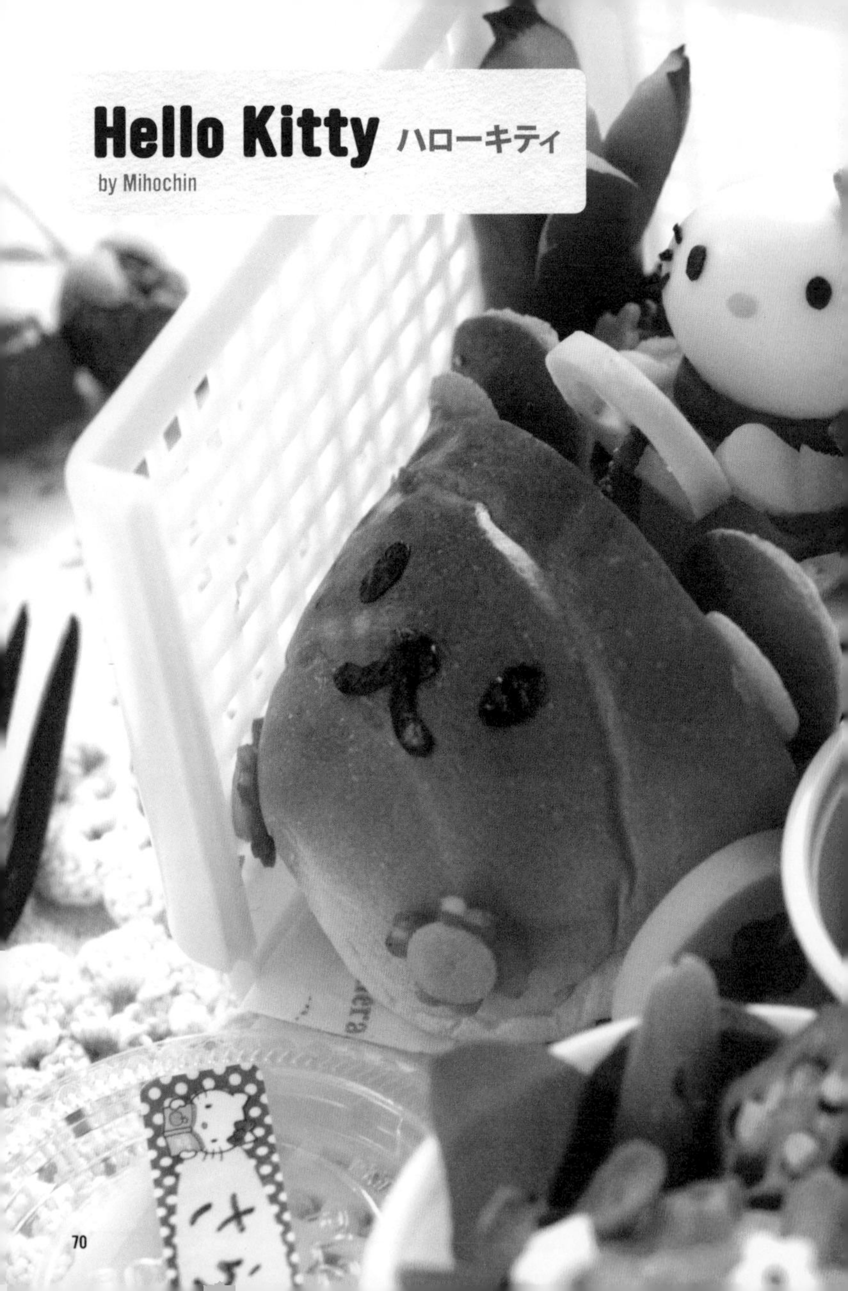

HELLO KITTY DRIVING

Hello Kitty: boiled quail egg, imitation crab,
  fish cake, fish cake dyed with blue food coloring,
  ham, seaweed, thinly fried egg
Bear: meatball, fried egg dyed with ketchup,
  seaweed, thinly fried egg, fish sausage, baby corn
Car: bread, seaweed, thinly friend egg, ham
Tires: fish sausage, carrot
Steering wheel: fish sausage, fried pasta
Apple: cherry tomato, green bean
Gift box: cheese, imitation crab, broccoli, ham,
  sausage, pumpkin salad, carrot, strawberry

From the Puroland Theme Park to merchandise and
shops across the globe, Sanrio's Hello Kitty character has been one of Japan's biggest exports since she
premiered in 1974.

Mihochin outdoes herself with this ode to Sanrio. A
sketch doesn't do this bento justice—you really need
the photograph (and/or skill) to put it all together.
Just try to duplicate it, I dare you!

GLOSSARY OF JAPANESE TERMS & INGREDIENT HOW-TO

キャラ弁作りの道具

HERE YOU WILL FIND A LIST OF JAPANESE ITEMS COMMONLY FOUND IN BENTOS, AS WELL AS RECIPES FOR SOME TYPICAL ITEMS, INCLUDING THOSE FOUND IN THE *CHARABEN* OF THIS BOOK.

BARAN

Have you ever ordered sushi and wondered if there is a name for the plastic green decorative grass? Well there is: *baran*.

BENTO BOX

A single-portion takeout or home-packed meal, made to fit into a box, which can vary in shape and form. Traditionally this consists of rice, fish or meat and one or more pickled or cooked vegetables as a side dish.

BULL-DOG SAUCE

This thick, savory sauce is like a semi-gelatinous Worcestershire with a soy zing.

CHARABEN

An elaborately arranged bento box, with food made into shapes resembling pop culture icons, people, animals or characters and items from nature.

DASHI

Japanese fish stock made by boiling *kombu* (kelp) and *katsuobushi* shavings (or bonito flakes). Dashi is the base of miso soup.

EDAMAME

Baby soybeans steamed or boiled in their pods, usually salted. Perfect with beer!

EGGS (DYED)

Food coloring is a quick and easy way to dye eggs, but it's better to find natural alternatives.

For each dye job, leave the eggs in the colored water for 10-20 minutes—the end result all depends on the time spent underwater, so experiment.
  yellow: curry powder or turmeric
  pink: purple cabbage and vinegar or
    beet juice
  blue: purple cabbage
  red/orange: annatto
  green: spinach powder
Other natural dyes include: betanin, cochineal, elderberry juice, paprika, saffron.

EGGS (HARD-BOILED)

It's not quite as easy as boiling water, but if you can do that, you can hard-boil eggs. You want a big pot of cold water. Fill up the water high enough so there is at least an inch of it covering the eggs. Place the eggs in the pot, making certain not to crowd them. Turn on the burner, cover the pot and let the water come to a nice rolling boil. When it does, turn off the burner and let the eggs sit on the burner for about 20 minutes, covered.

While all that's going on, prepare an ice bath in a bowl. After the eggs have rested in the hot water for 20 minutes move them to the ice bath and let them sit in the refrigerator for 20 minutes.

Have 20 minutes passed? If so, the eggs are ready to be peeled, sliced and diced!

FURIKAKE

A dry or semi-dry condiment sprinkled on rice. Typical ingredients include dried fish, seaweed, vegetables, sesame seeds, salt, sugar, chili flakes and MSG. While a variety of packaged *furikake* is readily available it is easy to make your own, depending on what flavors you like most.

HASHI YASUME

Literally "chopstick rest" this refers to a specific category of *ozaku*. These side dishes are meant to contrast with the flavor, texture and temperature of the main components of the meal. Pickled vegetables and cold salads are two common examples of *hashi yasume*.

KANIKAMA

Imitation crab.

KARE

The Japanese love their thicker, sweeter take on the traditional Indian curry. Most folks buy boxed Japanese curry roux, using vegetables, a protein of choice and rice to round out the meal. If you make your own from scratch, follow a traditional curry recipe and add apples, honey and a flour and oil roux to achieve that sweet thickness.

KAMABOKO
Fish cake.

HAMBURG (JAPANESE STYLE)
It's similar to Salisbury steak.
  1 lb ground beef
  1 egg
  2 slices of bread or 1/2 cup of panko
  1/2 onion (chopped)
  1/5 cup milk
  2/3 cup ketchup
  1/4 cup Bull-Dog Sauce or other
    BBQ sauce
  1 1/2 tbsp soy sauce
  3 tbsp sugar
Tear the bread up into small bits. You can use panko if you like, but I prefer whole wheat that is slightly stale. Place everything in a bowl and mix well.

Shape each hamburg into an oval patty, and pat it a few times with your hands to remove the air from the inside. Push down in the center of the patty with your finger.

With a little bit of oil, pan-fry the patties over medium-high heat until both sides are brown. Use a toothpick or fork to test the inside of the patty to see if it's done.

And that's it—you're ready. To be eaten plain, with ketchup or BBQ sauce!

HIJIKI
A high-fiber versatile seaweed often stewed with dashi and root vegetables.

KOROKKE
Japan's take on potato croquettes, these patties are made from a mixture of mashed potatoes and an ingredient (meat and/or vegetable) which is battered then deep-fried.

JOHBISAI/JOUBISAI
This is your stash of bento staples that stores well and can be easily added without too much preparation, like *furikake*, pickles, various dried seaweed and cured meats.

KYARABEN
An alternative spelling for *charaben*.

MEATBALLS
Meatballs in Japan often get slicked with a sweet and salty sauce. There are so many variations, but a good base is water, mirin, sake, light soy sauce and a bit of dissolved cornstarch. If you can stand the heat, add a few squirts of Sriracha.

Cook your meatballs in a pan. When they are done, remove them and then combine the sauce ingredients in the same pan, cooking it until it thickens up and reduces a bit. Once the sauce achieves the desired flavor and consistency return the meatballs to the pan and let them get happy in the sauce.
  veggie meatballs: pecans, garlic, panko,
    carrot, onion, egg, soy sauce,
    black pepper
  pork meatballs: garlic, panko, carrot,
    onion, soy sauce, black pepper

NIMAME
Use the bean of your choice to make these sweet simmered legumes. Cook 2 cups of beans as usual, but as they become tender add 1/4 cup sugar. Simmer for about 30 minutes and then add 1 tbsp of soy sauce and some honey to taste. Let cook for another 15 minutes and then you have a sweet complement to any bento.

NOODLES
Japanese noodles fit two different categories (basically), those made with wheat—ramen, somen and udon—and those made with buckwheat, like soba. One major exception is *shirataki* noodles, which are gummy, translucent and made from the konjac plant, or tofu.

NORI
An edible seaweed, typically used as a wrap for sushi and *onigiri*.

OBENTO SHEET
An obento sheet is a store-bought, edible sheet that comes in three colors: yellow (egg), orange (carrot), green (spinach). It's thin and quite durable, and used often in *charaben* for anime/manga characters. Here is a homemade version of the egg sheet:
  1 egg
  1/2 tbsp corn starch
Beat the egg well. In another bowl, combine 1 tbsp of water with cornstarch and stir well. Add this to your beaten egg and mix. Heat a pan with just a touch of oil, making sure the oil is spread evenly across the pan, removing any excess. Pour the mixture into the pan and spread evenly.

Once you're able to peel off the edge, slightly use a toothpick to gently loosen the edge all around. Flip the egg (I use my fingers—very carefully!) and keep on low heat another 10 seconds.

The best thing is you can wrap these and freeze them, so your bento will be a little easier to make in the morning! (To defrost just leave them at room temperature for a few minutes.)

OKAZU
This is a word that refers to the protein or vegetables that come with the rice during a meal.

ONIGIRI
You've cooked rice—now you can make rice balls! The rice is hot and sticky. Let it cool a bit, but not too much. Everything will hold together better if you form it when the rice is still warm. When making *onigiri* you want to have a bowl of water at the ready. Dipping your hands into the water will help with the heat and, more important, it will help keep the rice from sticking to your hands.

Adding a mixture of salt, rice vinegar and water to the rice can also help with keeping the rice nice and sticky. This is not necessary and the amount depends on how much rice you've made. All I can say is that you don't want to add too much.

Depending on what kind of *onigiri* you are making, letting the rice cool for a minute gives you time to work on any fillings.

If your *onigiri* has no fillings, just shape it using your wet hands. Pretend you're working playdough. Palm a clump of rice, making sure it isn't too much for your hands to handle, and shape it as necessary. It isn't rocket science but it does require some practice.

If you are putting a tasty treat inside the *onigiri* create a crater in the rice, using your thumb. It shouldn't be too big and it shouldn't be too deep. Fill the crater, cover it with rice and then finalize the *onigiri's* shape.

For the purpose of *charaben*, ornament your *onigiri* as instructed.

PANKO
Japanese breadcrumbs—panko—are a staple of the country's cuisine. Coarser than Western breadcrumbs and typically made from bread without crust, the increased surface area makes for a toothy crunch. You can pass the protein of your choice through an egg wash and then dredge it—chicken or pork cutlet, tofu, veggies—in panko and throw it in the frying pan. Because panko really is just breadcrumbs, you can jazz it up with the seasonings of your choice.

You can also make your own. Stale bread works best, but if you are using fresh bread leave it out for a few hours before putting it in the food processor.

RADISH (PICKLED)

If you've been around a bento or two you've noticed those cute little pink things...Well, those are sweet and sour pickled radishes, and they're a breeze to make.

    4 tbsp rice vinegar
    1 1/2 tbsp sugar
    1/2 tsp lemon juice

You can just double, triple, quadruple the measurements according to how much radish you have.

Cut the radish into 4 or more pieces. Sprinkle with salt and seal within an airtight bag for at least 30 minutes, refrigerated, to remove any excess water. Mix all ingredients into a jar. When ready, take the radish and use a paper towel to squeeze out any water that might still be inside. Then jar it up and be ready to eat it up the following day!

RICE

Okay, rice—the essence of Japanese food (and culture for that matter, but that's another topic for another book). In Japan, almost everyone cooks rice with a rice cooker. Rice has been a staple in Japan for over 2,000 years and they didn't have rice cookers back then. But with all that history you better believe that the Japanese are pretty serious about cooking rice.

For the sake of these recipes, if you don't use the right kind of rice and prepare it properly it simply won't behave. You can't make rice balls or sushi using long grain rice. Trust me on this!

Japanese rice (*gohan*) is basically white, short grain rice. You want to work on a 1:1 ratio of rice to water in order to make nice sticky rice that can be shaped easily.

Before you cook the rice you want to rinse it thoroughly, rubbing the grains together with your hands in water until the water turns cloudy. When it does, drain the water and rinse the rice again. Once the rice is rinsed, drain it and then let it sit in the water for a while. Again, this helps ensure that the rice comes out nice and sticky.

If you are using a rice cooker, now is the time to let the machine work its magic, giving you ample time to do other prep work.

If you are cooking the rice in a pot on the stove now is the time to turn on the heat, and place the lid on the pot. Bring the rice to a boil and then lower the heat, letting the rice simmer, covered, for 10-15 minutes. If you want to steal a quick peek do it now. The water should be pretty much gone, meaning it's time to turn off the burner, cover the pot and just let the rice steam to a finish.

For *onigiri* you want to work with the rice when it's still warm and sticky.

RICE (DYE)

Like with eggs, you can use food coloring if you don't feel like going about it with natural dyes, but why would you do that? Here are a few examples:

    yellow: curry powder, or turmeric. You can add varying amounts of ketchup to make it a richer yellow/orange
    black/gray: black sesame seed (freshly ground) and salt
    pink: beet juice

SOBORO

This simple meat mixture is a staple of bentos, and served over rice.

    1/2 lb ground beef/pork/chicken
    2 tbsp soy sauce
    1 tbsp sugar
    1 tbsp cooking sake or white wine

Cook the meat in a frying pan, breaking up any large chunks. Once cooked, turn the heat to low, mix in your ingredients and let simmer for a few minutes.

SASHIMI
Fresh raw fish (sliced thin) served with a dipping sauce.

SHOYU
Soy sauce.

SHUMAI DUMPLINGS
Filled with ground pork or shrimp or scallops or anything else you can fit into these little steamed purses of flavor, *shumai* can be eaten hot or at room tempurature. The wrappers consist of little more than flour, water and salt, but packaged ones are easy to come by. Soy sauce-based dipping sauces, usually including sesame oil, rice wine vinegar and sugar, often serve as condiment.

SUSHI
Vinegar rice topped with other ingredients, typically fish.

TAKOYAKI (AKA OCTOPUS BALLS)
A spherical, fried dumpling of batter with a piece of octopus inside, typically found as street food. I call these "Octopus Balls" because that's how an old man in Shinjuku's Golden Gai described them.

TAMAGO
Tamago is the Japanese word for egg. In English it is often used in the context of sushi but the slightly sweet, omelet atop rice is really *tamagoyaki*—fried egg. Even more so than shaping *onigiri*, this is a process that requires practice and patience.

If you have a rectangular frying pan that is ideal, but any non-stick frying pan works, though you will have to adjust measurements because making *tamagoyaki* requires room in the pan.

Lightly beat 4 eggs and then add a pinch of salt, a teaspoon of mirin, 1/2 teaspoon of soy sauce and 2 tablespoons of sugar. Some recipes swap dashi—a soup base of kombu seaweed, bonito flakes and dried shitake mushrooms—for mirin and soy sauce.

Put your pan over medium-low heat and oil it with vegetable/canola oil. Pour a layer of the egg mixture into the pan—a thin layer. When the edges begin to set use a spatula to roll the eggs, starting from the front of the pan. It doesn't matter that the eggs are not completely cooked. After you roll the eggs you should have some free real estate in the pan.

Using a paper towel, clean the empty portion of the pan and then add a little more oil. Add more of the egg mixture. Let it cook until the edges begin to set and then roll the eggs from the back of the pan over the new layer of eggs.

Repeat this process until you are out of the egg mixture.

The end result should be an egg log of sorts. Don't worry if it is slightly browned. If you have a bamboo sushi mat, roll the egg log in there, squeeze out any excess liquid and then let it cool. From there you slice and arrange and, eventually, eat!

TEMPURA
Deep-fried seafood and veggies—that's *amore!* Oh, wait, no, that's tempura. Almost as good as love. The key to making the batter is using cold water, really cold, ice cold. In fact, feel free to mix your flour and egg into ice water. Use one egg and equal parts water and flour. Some people use seltzer (something about the bubbles adds a lightness to the batter). The use of rice flour is another common variation to the batter.

Whisk the batter together and wait for your oil (peanut or some other suitable frying oil like canola) to reach 350-360 degrees. Once the oil is hot, dip the food into the batter and let it fry.

Vegetables will take longer than shrimp, and if you want your veggies to actually cook, cut them thin.

TERIYAKI
Grilled, broiled or pan-fried meat, fish, chicken or vegetables glazed with a sweet-ened soy sauce.

UMEBOSHI
Pickled ume fruit, similar to the apricot.

UNAGI
Grilled and flavored eel.

TAIYAKI
A fish-shaped cake made from waffle or pancake batter stuffed with sweet red bean paste, custard, chocolate or, at times, something savory.

YAKITORI
Barbecued chicken skewers, usually served with beer.

WASABI
Japanese horseradish, this root grows wild in Japan. If bought as a root it requires grating. It also comes in powder form or in a tube (typically processed with food color-ing).

ありがとうございました!

THE AUTHOR WOULD LIKE TO THANK

ERI HAMAJI, TAMARA ARELLANO, BUZZ POOLE, MARK BATTY, RAN LEE,
CAROLYN FRISCH, JAKE DAVIS, CALBEE POTATO SNACKS, ASAHI SUPER DRY
AND EVERYONE WHO CONTRIBUTED TO THIS BOOK.

WITHOUT YOU THERE WOULD ONLY BE VENDING MACHINES.

ABOUT
THE AUTHOR

著者について

CHRISTOPHER D SALYERS is a Brooklyn-based writer and book designer. He is the author of *Face Food* and *Vending Machines: Coined Consumerism*. You can keep up-to-date with the *charaben* world via his blog at www.facefoodbento.blogspot.com